HOW TO PLAY

KILL

2019 By Tony R. Smith. All Right Reserved

No part of this publication may be reproduced, distributed, or transmitted in any form or by any means, including photocopying, recording, or other electronic or mechanical methods, or by any information storage and retrieval system without the prior written permission of SSP, except in the case of very brief quotations embodied in critical reviews and certain other noncommercial uses permitted by copyright law.

TABLE OF CONTENTS

- INTRODUCTION 3
- CHAPTER ONE 6
  - HISTORY OF SOCCER 6
  - HOW TO PLAY SOCCER - SOCCER RULES 12
  - FUNDAMENTAL SOCCER RULES 16
  - SOCCER BALL CONTROL 19
  - CHAPTER TWO 22
- INSTRUCTIONS TO PLAY SOCCER - BALL CONTROL 22
- HOW TO IMPROVE YOUR SOCCER SKILLS 26
- 5 ESSENTIAL SOCCER SKILLS IN 5 MINUTES 30
  - HOW TO SCORE MORE SOCCER GOALS 34
- CHAPTER THREE 44
- COACHING SOCCER - ASSIGNING OFFENSIVE POSITIONS 44
- SOCCER OFFENSE - TIPS FOR SELECTING AN ATTACKING STYLE FOR RECREATIONAL SOCCER TEAMS 49
- HOW TO IMPROVE YOUR SOCCER DRIBBLING SKILLS 55
- TIPS TO INCREASE YOU SOCCER STRENGTH TRAINING 65
- RULES FOR PARENTS 69
- ACTIVITIES FOR CHILDREN AND ADOLESCENTS 81
- SPORTS INJURIES AND YOUR CHILD 85

INTRODUCTION

There are many things you can do with soccer balls. You can kick them. You can play get with them. You can hit them forward and in invert over the floor with a youth. You can spill them with your knees. You can skip soccer balls off your head. You can play evade ball with them. You can play your soccer balls in a pool. Or then again, you can play soccer with your soccer balls. Whatever your inclinations, you can discover something to do with a soccer ball.

The fascinating thing about soccer balls is that you needn't waste time with whatever else to play around with them. If you are are going to play soccer, at that point you may need some soccer objectives, or a soccer field to play on, yet you can, as a rule, discover a recreation center that has a few or you can make some yourself. More often than not, be that as it may, you needn't bother with some other equipment to discover things to do with merely your soccer ball.

You can kick soccer balls around for an extended period at some random minute and not get depleted with it. You can practice different sorts of kicks and soccer traps, and show them off to your allies. You can kick the soccer ball forward and in reverse with a buddy. You can kick your soccer ball around in diversion focus, a field, an estate, up in the mountains, on rocks, wherever you can't avoid being, you can kick a soccer ball around for fervor.

One beautiful thing about a soccer ball is that you can play diversions where you rival yourself. You can test yourself to see how regularly you can kick the soccer ball into the air without it hitting the ground, like a hacky sack. You can do it without any other person's information or with colleagues. You can bounce back it on your head for whatever time allotment that you can. You can spill it off your feet and your knees, your shoulders, and your head. When you've done it, you can continue endeavoring to improve and improve. Continue attempting to expand the occasions you can kick it, knee it, or hit it with your head without giving the soccer a chance to ball contact the ground. It's decent because it likewise causes you to build up your soccer abilities, just as merely being something enjoyable to do. You figure out how to have better ball control and when you are playing a diversion you can control the ball better as you are spilling down the field or going to your partners. It will assist you with dribbling past your rivals better. When you are in amusement, you additionally might be bound to complete a cool move or score a chill objective by hitting it your head into the aim.

CHAPTER ONE
History of Soccer

If you need to comprehend the historical backdrop of soccer, you need to concede that for reasons unknown, people have a natural urge to kick things. Regardless of whether it's to discharge dissatisfaction, or just for the sake of entertainment, we do this even without taking note.

How often have you not strolled in the city as a child (and not just), basically kicking that stone or cone on the ground before you out of weariness? It's this natural urge that remains at the premise of the historical backdrop of soccer.

- **When was soccer imagined?**

When talking about the historical backdrop of soccer, many individuals view England as the spot that soccer was conceived and in spite of the fact that this could be a genuine explanation in a specific setting, actually the English were the first to compose soccer around 1863, anyway they didn't "imagine" it per state. So on the off chance that 1863 is the year the game got "purified through water," at that point what year was soccer imagined and where?

Since soccer or soccer-like sports can be followed the path back to antiquated occasions, it's hard to stick point a particular year, yet history specialists of the wonder generally slash it down into three timeframes.

- **History of soccer amid old occasions**

While their fathers were off at war, kids would regularly snatch a fixed up cowhide ball, hit the adjacent field and begin a "war" on the ground. The absence of principles usually lead to battles, and genuine wounds and the game was viewed as risky in numerous areas.

A clear case of this can be found in the London British Museum, where an etching demonstrates a gathering of men attempting to win a cowhide ball, with a second picture showing a man with a broken arm. You figure it out.

- **Modern-day soccer**

As referenced above, although we didn't have the foggiest idea when soccer was concocted, we do know when it was sorted out as a game under a flexible arrangement of guidelines. Being a prominent practice in England, soccer was played clamorously, and customarily it would prompt the equivalent on and off-pitch fights like the ones happening amid medieval soccer matches. On each game, the two groups would concede to a specific arrangement of guidelines, yet with the absence of a ref contentions would regularly start up.

To maintain things in control, a couple of English clubs met in London on October 26, 1863, to make a lot of well-characterized and widespread standards for the amusement.

The Football Association was conceived, and even though their arrangement of principles did not make a difference to all clubs promptly, in a couple of decades, as soccer clubs changed from crudeness to polished methodology, their laws and direct limitations ended up a standard for everybody.

As should be obvious, there's no "right" approach to answer the "When was soccer developed?" question and you'll have a lot of contentions close by paying little heed to what period you accept was the sparkle that caused the rapidly spreading fire that soccer is today.

What's more, you'll most likely concur with me on this current: it's not by any stretch of the imagination that essential to know when soccer was concocted, but instead recognize that we are fortunate to have the capacity to appreciate this awesome game taking care of business, as we can in present day times.

How to Play Soccer - Soccer Rules

Soccer rules are misleadingly straightforward. The Laws of the Game, still intensely dependent on their forerunners from the 1860s, oversee this game worldwide, and even though the complexities can be unpredictable, you can become familiar with the essentials in actually minutes of viewing the Beautiful Game.

Soccer has many rules/laws. This impertinent term shows that there is something exceptionally erudite about the diversion, even though the original Laws record is only a couple of pages since quite a while ago contrasted with some different games. These rules are accessible using FIFA for any player to peruse for nothing.

The initial four of soccer's Laws of the Game identify with the mechanics. They portray the elements of the field (which can differ contingent upon whose arena you're at), the ball (which can likewise fluctuate between 27-28 crawls in boundary), the players (eleven for every group), and what the players can wear (soccer pullovers, soccer shorts, soccer socks, soccer boots/spikes, and compulsory shin cushions.)

Laws five and six diagrams the forces and duties of the arbitrators and his aides (the last of which are not obligatory in all alliances, yet are found in master soccer the world over.) After that, how the amusement is begun and ended (when the official identifies an infraction, or when the ball leaves play, or when an objective is scored) are taken a gander at in-laws seven through ten.

At that point comes soccer's offside standard, a Law so petulant it has its one of a kind number: eleven. The wrong guideline in soccer can be challenging to get, yet the nuts and bolts are this: if a player holds up almost a rival's objective with less than two adversaries among him and the goal line, and the ball is played to him, he is submitting an offside offense. This is 99% of cases implies that if a striker has just the goalkeeper to beat when the ball is kicked towards him, he will be hailed offside. (Obviously, if he gets the ball inside and, at that point runs one-on-one with the 'attendant, he didn't do anything's incorrect - and will most likely score!)

Laws twelve directly through to the last one - seventeen - clarify why the diversion may be halted for a foul, and what happens when this happens (a free-kick, either immediate or backhanded, contingent upon the seriousness of the offense; or even an extra shot one-on-one with the goalkeeper), and furthermore how toss-ins, objective kicks, and corner kicks work.

Best of all, you can peruse these laws in an evening and get the nuts and bolts that rapidly. In any case, the ideal method for all is to watch a soccer match-up with the laws in your grasp and allude to them as required. You'll be a soccer master in a matter of seconds.

There are different types of soccer, running from smaller scale soccer (3 aside) to the standard round of 11 alone. FIFA is the worldwide governing body for soccer, and it is FIFA who control the laws of the amusement that manage how to play soccer from a rules point of view, so visit the FIFA site to get a duplicate of the rules and begin learning the rules.

Fundamental Soccer Rules

Basic soccer rules are straightforward to pursue, the group that scores the most objectives wins!

Each group will comprise of 11 beginning players of which there are one goalkeeper and ten outfield players. The diversion will be played on a soccer pitch, and the field measurement will typically be a little more than 100 yards in length even though it could be shorter if it is a young soccer match-up.

Soccer crews are ordinarily part into arrangements comprising of guard, goalkeeper, and advances. Each group will likewise assign a chief even though this job isn't as critical as different games, for example, cricket and rugby. The commander will begin the amusement by flipping a coin with the ref, and the triumphant skipper has the choice of choosing which way their group will shoot.

This can be a preference if there is a strong wind which could alter course when the groups achieve the second half.

Soccer match-ups comprise of two parts enduring 45 minutes each even though damage time is frequently added by the official to cover any stoppages. When the amusement is a container tie, a world glass last for instance then additional time will be played comprising of a further two 15 minute durations. If the groups are as yet level at this stage, the amusement will form into a punishment shoot with each group selecting five extra shot takers who will attempt and beat the goalkeeper from the punishment spot (12 yards) until one group wins.

Amid the diversion, the ref can alert players and issue yellow and red cards. Yellow cards are issued for minor or a genuine of fouls by a similar player which results in a booking, two yellow cards are issued, at that point, these equivalents a red card and the guilty player is sent off the field.

A straight red card can be additionally be issued for genuine unfairness or denying an adversary a goalscoring opportunity. Each group must have at least seven players on the field, so if one group have over five players sent off, at that point the amusement would be relinquished, this is uncommon yet has happened a couple of times in rough diversions!

A standout amongst the essential fundamental rules of soccer is the offside principle which mostly keeps attacking players from picking up an uncalled for preferred standpoint as when a pass is made there must be two resistance players closer to the objective than the assaulting player. If the assaulting player is level with a safeguard, at that point he is as yet onside so play proceeds. The official has two colleagues (recently known as linesman) on either side of the field to help judge the offside principle.

Soccer Ball Control

To figure out how to control soccer ball you have to comprehend that the ball has a significant association with you. The ball and you should be companions, and I don't imply that you should converse with the ball, however, handle it cautiously and with delicate and I guarantee that it will do as you wish.

You have most likely seen that when a soccer player sees a ball moving towards him/her, their quick response on this is to kick it with the hardest power they need to send the ball distant as could be expected under the circumstances. At that point, this equivalent player all of a sudden begins to pursue the ball as though they needed to apologize to the ball for kicking it 50 yards away.

Before I figured out how to control the ball, I additionally kicked it far as conceivable without reflecting over how or where the significant thing as I as of now have said is to kick the ball far as would be prudent. If you need to play soccer, at that point the main thing you should do is to figure out how to control the ball and in this way likewise control the heading if which you kick it.

Deftness and ball control in soccer is something that should be drilled. There are a few players that appear to have been brought into the world with excellent soccer control; however, they are not many. Pelé said once: To ace spryness and ball control in soccer you should treat the ball similarly as though was an individual, and that is with deference and comprehension.

Presently you most likely imagine that he should be high on medication or something, I mean what the hell would he say he is looking at, treating a ball like an individual? Please, offer me a reprieve. Before you click back in your program, let me disclose to you that key to ace soccer ball control you have to treat is much the same as if you were closest companions. Here are how to do it by and by (you don't have to talk with it : -)

Put it on the ground and take a gander at it. The ball will appear to inquire as to whether you need to come and play, isn't that right? Your body must be all around adjusted, and your muscles loose. At that point tenderly spot your foot over the ball and move it back, endeavoring to lift the ball from the beginning putting your toe under it. The more you hold the ball under your control, the better. To keep your parity, twist forward and keep your arms up, somewhat bowed and loose, only a little underneath the line of your shoulder.

CHAPTER TWO
Instructions to Play Soccer - Ball Control

Controlling the ball in soccer is a significant aptitude that is basic when you are figuring out how to play soccer. In simple terms, controlling the ball is the "basic" errand of accepting the ball and taking care of business the ball in a position that you need it for your best course of action. By and large, this implies taking care of business the ball on the ground and in a place where you can kick the ball with your favored foot toward the path that you wish to kick the ball. Basic, isn't that so?

Any piece of the body (except the hands and arm) can be utilized to control the ball. However, the fundamental body parts are the foot, thigh, middle (upper and lower) and head. I have here and there utilized the back of my legs as well, yet just in certain circumstances, which I will clarify later. Kick it into high gear. Behind the Ball, It doesn't generally make a difference what part of the body that is utilized, the strategy is the equivalent. As the ball is drawing closer, the player must modify their body position with the goal that they are prepared to get the shot. This implies on their toes and guaranteeing that as quite a bit of their body is "behind" the ball. It is essential to take care of business your body behind the ball for two fundamental reasons.

You will have a front on perspective on the ball as it approaches and in this way have an excellent view on the ball.

If you have misinterpreted the trip of the ball having a more significant amount of your behind the ball diminishes the danger of you not controlling the ball as the ball is probably going to interface with another piece of your body.

Body Position After taking care of business behind the ball, the player must consider the body position that is expected to control the ball so that the ball is coordinated where the player needs the ball to go. One good case of this is getting the player to "open up" or get the ball with an open body position, permitting the player see a greater amount of the playing field and to coordinate the ball forward, by accepting the ball with their back foot. The method of "opening up" and accepting the ball with an open position is significant, and one which must be instructed to your players. Whenever you are watching a broadcast amusement, merely listen and perceive how players position themselves while getting the ball.

Padding the ball The last part is the first contact of the body with the ball. This is the most significant piece of controlling the ball and needs precise execution. The procedure is to pad the ball with the goal that the ball does not bob off the players' body excessively far. To stuff the ball, essentially pull back the piece of the entity that is accepting the ball on effect, which "mollifies the blow" and guarantee that the ball remains inside reach of the player.

The Next Step One regular misstep when showing players how to play soccer is for players to be educated to stop the ball "dead" and directly before their foot. When you are figuring out how to control the ball, usually far superior to either have the ball moving toward the path that you need to go at a pace that keeps the ball inside your range and makes the ball prepared for your best course of action, regardless of whether that is a shot, a pass or to spill with the ball. Realizing how to control the ball and getting the opportunity to do what you need it to as fast as could be expected under the circumstances, gives you the edge over your adversaries.

Back of the Legs?

If the ball is originating from extraordinary tallness, at that point a unique method to control the ball is to utilize the back of the legs by "sitting" on the ball following it skips. This strategy is enjoyable but requires excellent planning to guarantee that you are in a sitting position, over the ball, at precisely the perfect time and in the correct spot. This system isn't regularly trained when showing players how to play soccer, yet it is a decent one and can be overpowering at the ideal time.

How to Improve Your Soccer Skills

If you ask a soccer coach what question they get asked the most, it will likely be "how might I improve my soccer skills?" A coach would tell you practice as much as possible.

Being a good player you needn't bother with your entire group or a whole soccer field to build your athletic capacities. All you need is a ball, a divider, and a little territory where you can have some very practice time. How about we investigate a couple of things that you can do to help improve your soccer skills:

1)Juggle - One of the best things that you can do to help improve your soccer capacities is to work on juggling the ball. For the individuals who are amateurs, this involves kicking the ball slightly into the air utilizing the highest point of your feet, your thighs, or your head (no hands!). For fledglings, begin by going for 1-3 juggles at any given moment. When you are further developed, you can work on juggling the ball the same number of times as you need.

2)Pass and shoot-While it is ideal for working on passing and shooting with a companion or colleague, you can likewise do it alone. To practice your skills use a good ball and a divider. Pass the ball to the divider. If there is a rebound, endeavor to recover control of your ball as fast as could be expected under the circumstances. If you need to work on giving, place a little bit of tape on the divider and work on your point, attempting to hit it with the ball.

3)Turns - There are six sharp turns in soccer; the stop turn, within snare, the Cruyff, the outside trap, the progression over, and the drag back. Work on acing each corner independently. When you have done as such, take a shot at various blends.

4)Moves - As you most likely know, there is a wide range of soccer moves that you can utilize. Since there are such a large number of, you don't have to realize how to play out every one of them. Start by picking two moves that you like and work on them until they are idealized (until you can perform them without considering). When you have idealized these moves, you can move on to find out additional. Make an effort not to become involved with adopting an excessive number of various movements immediately as you may finish up befuddling them up to come diversion time.

5) Control - To rehearse power, pick an open zone. Kick the ball noticeable all around and work on controlling it as it descends. Utilize your feet, chest, thighs, and head, controlling the ball with whichever part appears to be fit.

The above are only a couple of the numerous strategies that you can use to improve your soccer skills. If you are in a group or know somebody who wouldn't see any problems with rehearsing with you, welcome them to participate in a training session. Repeating with a divider can improve your skills; however, rehearsing with a partner can take your skills to the following dimension.

Continuously recollect - paying little mind to whether you are a tenderfoot or a specialist, practice is essential to improve and keep up your soccer skills.

5 Essential Soccer Skills in 5 Minutes

The sport of soccer is unquestionably an incredible diversion to play; however, without soccer skills, it can't be utterly delighted in. This doesn't imply that you need to spill around players like Lionel Messi or curve it like Beckham. What it means, is that you should attempt to turn into the best player you can by improving your skills. Soccer requires many skills. However, 5 of them emerge from the rest.

Capacity To Kick

Is soccer extremely conceivable without kicking? It's outlandish. It's where the ball is moved from one end of the pitch to the next using a kicking movement. So there's no uncertainty this is the most significant expertise. Fortunately, everybody can kick, however, would everyone be able to kick accurately with reason? That is something you need to ace.

Capacity To Pass

A few people may contend that passing the ball is much the same as kicking the ball. I will, in general, oppose this idea. Kicking chiefly includes the top piece of the boot while passing mostly consists of the side of the boot. Passing is an expertise that requires more exactness than kicking. Passing is the way to understanding a play, provided that it isn't exact; at that point, it can separate a move.

Capacity To Trap

Numerous players consider passing or kicking the ball before getting the shot. Subsequently, when they do get the ball, many are not ready to control it, and they lose ownership. Therefore, catching is a standout amongst the most significant and helpful soccer skills to ace.

Capacity To Dribble

Who doesn't love watching players spill their way down the field, moving restriction players out of position and opening up spaces for their colleagues to score an objective? Incredible dribblers are among the most-appreciated soccer players, and spilling is a most valuable and wanted soccer expertise that anybody should endeavor to ace.

Capacity To Shoot

What's the purpose of having the capacity to kick, pass, trap and spill when you can't shoot at the objective? You may contend that you're not a striker. However, you may one day wind up in an objective scoring chance to win for your group. Shooting is undoubtedly significant soccer expertise. Furthermore, incidentally, who doesn't care for scoring?

Soccer is a fun and energizing amusement to play and it ought to dependably stay that way. In any case, by learning the five fundamental soccer skills laid out in this section, it tends to be considerably progressively fun and energizing.

How to Score More Soccer Goals

When it truly boils down to it, winning games is the best way to keep camaraderie high, and making more goals is essential to winning those games. How might you ensure your group scores more goals? Numerous coaches have discovered huge accomplishment by approaching the problem in a twofold way: expanding the number of shots, and expanding the accuracy of those shots. In any case, attitude can be similarly as significant. So what is a mentor who needs to fence his wagers to do?

1. Manage any attitude problems. Numerous soccer players, particularly the more youthful ones, won't endeavor to score notwithstanding when the open door presents. This is because of a simple attitude problem "they are alarmed of missing"! The best approach to manage this is to applaud each shot, paying little respect to the result. Stress that is attempting is what's most significant because nobody makes an objective easily. Additionally, don't enable different individuals from the group to grumble when a colleague misses a shot. Reveal to them it's smarter to miss than never have attempted, and establish a strategy of telling players "Decent attempt!" after any endeavor.

2. Manage certainty issues. Numerous players are not sure about their capacity to shoot and make the objective, so they stay away from it at each expense. This must be halted from developing in any way, and the best to do that is by customary practice. Instruct them to deal with the

ball skillfully and precisely, and they'll be bound to utilize their abilities on the field.

3.Instruct them to search for and abuse openings in the restricting protection. Is there a 'gap' that the objective guardian can't reach in time? Assuming this is the case, an opportunity to move is present! Utilizing great strategy head down, eyes, on the ball-the player should kick the ball and ideally score. If they make the objective, they are considerably more liable to attempt again next time.

4.Instruct them to shoot such that expands their odds of progress. This implies kicking the ball to the objective in a manner the goalie doesn't anticipate. Take a stab at kicking the ball lower or more distant to the other side, or even legitimately at the objective guardian. At the point when a shot is low and wide, the actual manager may finish up wrong-footed, giving your group one more score.

5.Work on making goals until it is second nature. With the end goal for this to work, the objective ought to be a similar size as the goals they will experience practically speaking and have a sensible number of protectors just as a goalie. At the point when kids become accustomed to approaching this somewhat intimidating setup and succeeding, they will almost certainly do likewise in real diversion play.

By improving attitude, raising the number of shots, and raising the accuracy of those shots, you ought to rapidly find that your number of goals increments by the amusement. Numerous coaches find that this sort of objective preparing has an exponentially positive effect; as more players endeavor and make goals, in addition to the fact that they are bound to attempt once more, yet their partners might also be roused!

Instructions to Increase Your Soccer IQ

What is soccer IQ and how might we use it to improve our amusement?

Soccer IQ is a term that characterizes how brilliant we are playing. We should think carefully when we are in that field. It does us a whole lot of nothing to keep running from player to player endeavoring to take care of business the ball. We merely go through the entirety of our vitality. Perhaps if you are playing against a lousy group, you could catch the ball keep running with the ball and possibly score an objective.

If you are confronting a brilliant adversary, they will pass the ball around you as though they are in training. You should figure out how to peruse the rival. Foresee their every move. If you can do that, you can ordinarily block the ball and compose a brisk assault and turn the entire match around.

You should get ready for a diversion. Concentrate your adversary's amusement before you venture on that field. Discover what the other group shortcomings and qualities are. Is their barrier lineup frail? Are their midfielders anxious when they get the ball? Do they have an eminent striker? Is their goalie any great? It doesn't have any effect if you are a player attempting to be the best in that field or a mentor setting up your group for an amusement. You should think carefully.

Soccer is considerably more than merely kicking the ball around. Get ready for your rival and concentrate everything they might do and diversion play. However, the most significant thing is that you set yourself up. Clear your head. Forget all the negative. Envision yourself as a standout amongst the best soccer player that ever venture on that field. Concentrate on your qualities, keep running on that field and abandon them puzzled.

If you could do that for each diversion, you are going to play, at that point you will before long find the intensity of soccer IQ. With cautious readiness and appropriate diversion technique, you can even beat the rivals that are a lot more grounded and snappier. Try not to misunderstand me. There is not a viable replacement for all the diligent work you put in on your training. In any case, on the other hand, it isn't all in merciless power.

An incredible case of that is Lionel Messi, who is moving beyond his adversaries smoothly. He peruses his adversaries, envisions everything they might do, moves beyond them and puts that ball in the top right corner.

Ground-breaking Tips and Secrets on How to Score Goals in Soccer (Football)

1) You need to need to Score Goals.

Each time you're on the ball, you should look score goals. If you take a gander at the best objective scorers on the planet, the Lionel Messi' and Cristiano Ronaldo's, each time they are on the ball the main thing at the forefront of their thoughts is to score. Their first touch is dependably towards the restriction's objective and there searching for open space to underwrite. Continuously hope to Score! It's an attitude the same amount of as it is a range of abilities.

2) Don't Hesitate with regards to the shooting.

An excessive number of players beat one player and get an opening, at that point merely pass the ball off to another player or trust that the protector will get back in position and endeavor to beat him/her once more. Shoot the ball! Try not to waver with regards to the shooting. You're never going to Score if you don't shoot. If you wind up hesitating when you have an open shot, see this propensity, and endeavor to address it after some time.

3) Get into Goal scoring zones.

You're not going to score many goals in case you're hanging out at the midway line. If you need to score goals, you need to get into the warmth of the activity. In fact you're a striker jump on the finish of through balls and crosses. Midfielders need to finish their runs and get into the crate. Protectors can even get forward to assist if the circumstance permits. You will score many goals in your career only by being in the right spot at the right time.

Continuously complete your run. Get into objective scoring zones!

4) Demand the ball when your open.

Tell colleagues that you're open. Tell them that you need the ball. Numerous players don't need the ball when they are free; they are frightened to take care of business the shot and have the weight on them to complete the objective. You have to expel this propensity from your amusement if this is as of now your circumstance. Be sure, request the ball, and take your risks. You'll never score if you don't attempt.

5) Always, Technique and Accuracy over power.

You are not going to score such vast numbers of goals as you could, if all you endeavor to do each time you get a shot, is crush the ball as hard as possible. I understand we as a whole need to tear a rankling chance into the top corner and put an entire in the back of the net - however help yourself out. Concentrate on accuracy and method before power; place the ball into an open zone of the objective as opposed to endeavoring to shoot the ball as hard as possible. Trust me; this will result in a lot more goals all through your Soccer career.

CHAPTER THREE
Coaching Soccer - Assigning Offensive Positions

It is debatable that halfbacks are intentionally intended for defense instead of offense. However, it can likewise be contended that such position can be used for hostile plays as halfbacks can slide in to advance positions. The change empowers them to be the lance purpose of any assault and maybe become the scorers themselves.

Halfbacks and midfielders ought to have precise information of the diversion's guarded angles and should view their situations as their group's rampart of defense.

Focus Halfback

Otherwise called the "boss" of the group, the inside halfback is viewed as the group's pinnacle of intensity in light of his impact and other physical traits that give him direction over his teammates. The middle halfback goes about as the focal protector who is slated to end any hostile activities by the other group by making convenient handles and block attempts. His fundamental task is the contradicting group's lead striker and must keep up inside his range to play viable defense. Physical qualities of a middle halfback incorporate stature, speed, quality, and stamina. Mentally, an inside halfback must possess tenacity, assertiveness, decisiveness, confidence, and self- control.

Midfielders

Midfielders, the playmakers of the group, are entrusted with the duty to arrange the offense plays. They set the pace, regardless of whether speed things up or back off, contingent upon the current states of the amusement. Midfielders must interface with their teammates to have the capacity to prevail with their course of action. If they are not in a state of harmony with different individuals from the group, this frequently prompts poor execution, lazy supporting players, and disorder.

A midfielder must apply a noticeable want to pick up possession. To do that, a midfielder ought to exceed expectations in various components, which involve stamina, quality, speed, aggressive battling soul, assurance, and confidence on and off the ball. For the most part, midfielders are those whose yield and work rate are more prominent than their teammates.

Wingers

The winger's position is a two-dimensional methodology - they can assault, and they can remain wide along the flanks to extend the defense. The winger likewise offers help to security. On most occasions, the winger is the most slender, littlest, and the least physically-forcing individual from the group. Wingers enormously rely upon their skill, speed, and master spilling abilities to avoid their defenders.

It is generally significant that wingers must possess an incredible level of confidence just as the heart to take on higher and increasingly forceful players. They should likewise have sharp learning on the standards of the width in the assault.

Advances/Strikers

The principal scorers of any soccer crew, the strikers, are the lead players in all-out attack mode end. Working connected at the hip, strikers regularly pivot their jobs as feeders and lead strikers and always check the contradicting group's defense for any imperfections and conceivable windows to score. For mentors who hope to relegate players to such positions, they should search for players who have talent in scoring and very little enthusiasm for boring any cautious assignments. Speed and quality are the two principle traits a striker ought to possess.

While in the amusement, strikers have their backs on the objective, which makes them defenseless to any guarded moves from behind. A striker like this must be mindful of his environment and the situation of the defenders.
Besides that, considering the level of defense that is set up close to the objective, a striker must probably ingest any types of discipline and possess a high edge for torment.

Soccer Offense - Tips For Selecting an Attacking Style For Recreational Soccer Teams

It is more enthusiastically to instruct soccer assaulting than soccer defense. It is simpler to have a decent soccer defense than a decent soccer offense since soccer defense is tied in with crushing (or disturbing) and soccer assaulting is tied in with making. Recreational soccer crews can have a better than average protection by basically putting extreme, forceful players close to the objective you are safeguarding and having them kick the ball away. Like this, the rival must begin the soccer assault once again each time and when your Midfielders or Forwards can win those cleared balls, at that point in addition to the fact that you have the opportunity to assault and score, yet you fend off the ball from the rival so the adversary can't score.

Then again, to score against a decent defense generally requires an organized exertion including a few players and quick soccer passing, spilling, collaboration and making the best decision at the opportune time. One mistake...one terrible pass...and the assault closes with the ball either kicked away or with the adversary picking up possession of the ball. What's more, regardless of whether the attackers are successful in drawing sufficiently near for a not too bad shot, the ball should, in any case, move beyond the Goalkeeper and go into the objective for a score.

Be sensible. When choosing which Attacking Style to show your group, you should be practical, or you will be disillusioned, your group will end up disappointed, you will be unsuccessful, and nobody will have a ton of fun. Give me a chance to utilize a similarity: If you choose you to need to figure out how to juggle tennis balls using your hands, you will initially begin with a couple of shots - you won't start with 4. I figured out how to juggle tennis balls and started with one, at that point two, at that point 3. I never got to 4 since I would not like to devote an opportunity to rehearse.

When choosing what Attacking Style you will show your group, you should be reasonable about your player's capacities, the number of powerless players you have in your group, and the measure of soccer training time you have. The Attacking Style you can effectively use with a group of every incredible player that rehearses 3 hours out of every week all year and has been as one for a year (e.g., a Travel group) will be not quite the same as the style you can successfully use with a Recreational group that has a blend of players (some great and some feeble) and just practices one hour out of each week.

Do you have any frail players?. Try not to expect a Recreational group that has powerless players and just practices once per week to have the capacity to play a similar Attacking Style as a Travel Team that has every incredible player and methods for 3 hours out of each

The goal is provided that you endeavor to utilize a Possession style of assault, delicate players resemble "feeble connections in a chain." I don't express this to be mean, to mention that it is a factor you should think about while picking an Attacking Style. If you have three players who can pass the ball and one who can't, a short passing assault won't work if it includes the player who can't move. This is the reason somehow, or other recreational mentors have a more strenuous activity than movement mentors, and the Attacking Style that is practical for a movement mentor probably won't be sensible for a recreational mentor.

A Possession assaulting style will possibly work if you have a fantastic group with no frail players. The perfect Attacking Style controls the ball when you attack. Since we realize that a player can't spill exceptionally far against great defenders, it would appear to be intelligent that the ideal approach to control the ball is bypassing it, and that is valid. That Attacking Style is known as a "Possession" style (or a short passing style or a "Roundabout" style). In a perfect world, the group with the ball would control the ball everywhere throughout the field, regardless of whether the ball is close to your objective (which is known as the "Guarded Third"). Many expert groups play along these lines. Regardless, it is also clear that not every single proficient group play along these lines, and not every National Team play like this. The reason is that it is hard to make bunches of successive short passes while under strain and if you turn over the ball close to your objective, your rival may score. Consider U.S. football...most of the time a group will punt on fourth down if they are inside their 35-yard line (which is their Defensive Third). The reason is that it is excessively hazardous if they somehow happened to turn over the ball there.

Here is my proposal: Use the Attacking Style that is reasonable for your group and that gives your group the most obvious opportunity to be successful. A few mentors figure they should attempt to show recreational players a "Possession" style of assault for the whole field. That is most likely doubtful for 99% of every single recreational group. Then again, most Rec groups can play an Attacking Style that utilizes long kicks (an "immediate" style) to take care of business the ball into their Attacking Third (the third of the field nearest to the rival's objective) or into the Attacking Half and afterward play a Possession style to the degree they are capable. I don't think you are harming anybody by utilizing this style and how I encourage you to instruct this is altogether different from simply kicking the ball hard - you can train your Midfielders and Forwards to move so they are in a position to win balls that are cleared by the Fullbacks. How do the Midfielders and Forwards realize where to position themselves? It is basic: Teach your Fullbacks to kick a "Lobbed Pass" straight ahead and show the Midfielders and Forwards to anticipate that and to position so they can win those balls. This is an Attacking Plan that is easy to instruct and can be utilized successfully by Rec groups. If a Rec player proceeds to play on a Travel group, the person in question will essentially become familiar with a progressively controlled Attacking Style around then. In any case, meanwhile they will have a great time and can become familiar with a ton, for example, appropriate strategy for a within foot pass, a propelled toss in, Passing to Space, Movement off the Ball, First Attacker/Second Attacker/Third Attacker, how to move to be in position to win cleared ball, hustling and playing hard, that they should position and battle to win the ball, and a Possession style of assault in the Attacking Third or Attacking Half. What's more, on defense mentors can show Shift and Sag (basically keeping up the shape and channeling for those of you who utilize those terms), First

Defender/Second Defender, denoting, zone defense and numerous different things.

How to Improve Your Soccer Dribbling Skills

Soccer is an extraordinary amusement to be played, but on the other hand, it's an incredible diversion to be viewed. Somebody curious about soccer may ponder what precisely it is that makes it the most prominent game on earth.

Much the same as the ball has its pummel dunks and back street oh no, baseball its grand slams or boxing its knockouts, soccer has a few key components that make it a very engaging amusement: objectives, passes, handles and spilling.

It's the last one that I esteem most, since I trust that a decent spill isn't just staggering, however, it tends to be amazingly effective in an amusement, so I will devote the accompanying article to clarifying how soccer spilling functions, how you can prepare it, center around two or three unique spilling moves and see what soccer capacities influence your spelling ability.

Soccer Dribbling - Introduction to the World of Ankle Breakers

By definition, soccer spilling is a strategy utilized by the ball transporter to pass the ball past a direct rival, without yielding possession. This might be a firm word reference like a statement, yet in truth, soccer spilling is as straightforward an the idea like that: do anything you can (in the limits of the soccer laws) to move beyond your rival and keep possession of the ball. Moving beyond your adversary" needs a bit of clarifying.

At a first look, that may appear to be confined to vertically outperforming your adversary on the pitch, when in truth spilling should be possible sideways, or even back towards your very own half (when you need to maintain a strategic distance from a handle for instance) and by and large it's only a methods for clearing up the space to get a pass or shot in. This doesn't take care of business the ball on the opposite side of your rival, yet it avoids him, enabling you to proceed with the play to your colleagues.

Soccer Dribbling - Types of Dribbles

There are a few kinds of spills that have different purposes in the amusement, and by sorts of spills I don't mean explicit moves or explicit traps, but instead diversion mechanics including spills that have a specific real objective.

Weight Avoiding Dribbles - This is likely the most widely recognized kind of spill in the diversion and as a focal midfielder pretty much every bit of the ball you persuade should be trailed by a weight-maintaining a strategic distance from the spill. This includes a quick flick of the ball in a region with some space while being experiencing tension from a rival, and its objective is to give you a couple of moments to execute a pass, or now and again a shot.

The most significant part of weight maintaining a strategic distance from spills is realizing where you're going to move the ball even before you get to it. Think about that you will most likely have two or three seconds to pass or shoot the ball after such a spill since the protector will rush to position himself before the ball once more, or attempt to handle you conclusively.

Extraordinary instances of players who utilize this sort of spill adequately incorporate Ronaldinho, Clarence Seedorf or Michael Ballack.

Speed Dribbles - Speed spills are generally prevalent with wing-backs since the sides usually are progressively open and free and they enable a quick player to for all intents and purposes to toss the ball forward and keep running for it once more, smoking a couple of rivals all the while.

Speed spills aren't extravagant as far as ball control, anyway the dribbler needs to concentrate on pushing the ball forward, so he doesn't lose possession to a contradicting safeguard or toss the ball out of the playing securities. A couple of instances of extraordinary speed dribblers incorporate Arjen Robben, Cristiano Ronaldo, Marc Overmars or Dani Alves.

Getting Dribbles - This is likely a standout amongst the best approaches to spill, yet it can likewise be the hardest: circumventing your rival straight from accepting the ball. It can startle complete protection and make destruction for the contradicting group, yet you genuinely must be a talented player to create extraordinary accepting spills.

As an issue of first significance, you need a unique vision on the pitch, knowing precisely where your rivals are and where you can locate some open space on the field, even before the ball gets to your foot.

Furthermore, you should be an ideal control of the ball accepting strategy, since pushing it excessively delicate or too hard will destroy the spill. To wrap things up, you have to utilize your body to trap your immediate rival reeling, enabling you to transform what's more, push the ball into open space unhindered.

Soccer Dribbling - Skill Factors Involved in Dribbles

You've likely enticed to state that ball control is the primary expertise engaged with spilling, yet in truth, there are significantly more factors that should be included for a useful spill. How about we take them well ordered:

Ball Control - Indeed, ball control is a general rule that is required for practically a wide range of spills. Ball control is the capacity to move with the ball, without losing possession, so it virtually expects you to know how difficult to hit the ball while pushing ahead with it, just as sorting out your body development, so that enables you to progress and get this show on the road the ball to your feet once more.

Ball control likewise alludes to having the capacity to trap or get a ball without pushing it excessively further far from your body, which, for our situation, is amazingly valuable in getting spills. Ball control is significant for a wide range of players when spilling, paying little heed to their position on the pitch.

Quality - Strength is a central point in accepting spills and positional ones, since it enables you to utilize your body as a divider between the ball and your adversary, repositioning the person in question, so you make leeway towards the foe objective.

If you take a gander at a portion of the players that are viewed as the best spills out there these days, for example,

Ronaldinho or Zinedine Zidane, you'll see that they all the time utilize their body in spills, so as to outperform an adversary or alleviate themselves of weight and discover a pass or a shot.

In what respects soccer spilling, quality is for the most part significant for focal midfielders, who are under steady weight from the contradicting group and for aggressors who should utilize their bodies to shield the ball before they can release a spill in the case.

Speed - Being quicker than your rival is a specific something, yet realizing how to get this show on the road the ball past him AND recover possession is the way to a useful speed spill. On the off chance that the speed contrast is extraordinarily in support of the aggressor, he can drive the ball forward along the contribute an unfilled zone and keep running for it.

If space is restricted, or if the speed contrast isn't so incredible between the ball transporter and the safeguard, the minute you begin the spill is critical.

You have to begin increasing the pace when the safeguard is wobbly (perhaps after you startle him with development from your body) and ensure you have enough space to move around him.

Flimsier Foot Ability - Dribbles regularly include utilizing the two feet and different pieces of the foot (the underside, the instep, the backheel, the front, the outside or within) to work appropriately, and your more fragile foot can frequently cause you issues.

Being uncertain of your more fragile foot will abandon you entirely helpless before an astute safeguard since he'll know there's only one course you can spill towards utilizing your stable foot.

Soccer Dribbling - Training Your Dribbling Skill

You can prepare spilling separately, with a colleague or in a group. Exclusively, you can set up an obstacle course, at that point wave your way through the obstacles like a skier would through banners. Ensure you utilize the two feet, so you figure out how to spill toward every path and to use your more fragile foot also.

Matching up with a partner is likewise an incredible method to rehearse your soccer spilling. This strategy has two points of interest: as a matter of first importance, it enables you to prepare your spills against a genuine adversary, which changes very a few parameters by the way you train in contrast with keeping away from ground obstacles.

Besides, expecting you change jobs with your colleague from time to time, enabling him to turn into the dribbler, you will likewise go about as a protector and will figure out how safeguards think when adapting to a rival's spill.

Knowing your "adversary" will enable you to peruse your match adversaries like an open book, and you'll before long recognize what to do in any match circumstance where a spill is required.

Group spilling instructional courses for the most part center on weight staying away from spills as opposed to independently circumventing a solitary adversary. Rehearsing in a group simulates match conditions best, and it's a powerful method to work out your spilling expertise usually, instead of constrained as you would have with an individual or combined preparing.

Tips to Increase You Soccer Strength Training

If you are keen on improving your soccer strength training routine? If you want to play soccer, you may take a shot at this frequently. The way to being a great soccer player is having a ton of strength, just as stamina and these aren't merely going to occur without any forethought either.

You'll need to assume responsibility for improving as a soccer player all alone because nobody else can do it for you. One of the essential criteria you ought to want to get more perseverance to make you a superior player. This will push you through those grueling workouts and enable you to see that soccer strength training is a need to turning into a great player.

Soccer requests an abnormal state of stamina, and you should work at a strength training soccer program to enable you to help your perseverance as much as you can. This will require much diligent work just as a commitment on your part, yet if you need it sufficiently terrible you can be the most significant player in the group.

Additionally, you won't just form you soccer stamina; however, you'll assemble your certainty also. Just envision your adversaries being depleted while despite everything you're going solid. This is a good motivator too to enable you to proceed with the strength training required to make you a superior soccer player.

Recorded underneath are some great exercises to help you construct that soccer strength that can enable you to have the best continuance in the group:

1. Take a stab at running set up for five minutes, at that point begin running for five moments, and afterward back it back off to a run for five additional minutes. This is a great soccer perseverance exercise that makes you more grounded and last longer also.

2. Complete a full body squat and utilize your whole weight while doing as such.

3.Have a go at completing 40 press-ups in one moment, and 40 squat push the next moment. This is a great soccer strength training exercise you ought to do day by day. Have a go at doing six days in a row and taking a couple of vacation days, at that point continuing it.

3.Attempt to twist and six-tenths of your body weight every day. This can truly help you in structure your soccer stamina.

The way to creating stamina you have to play soccer is to have a go at doing finish rounds of specific exercises at an increased dimension for particular timeframes. This will enable your body to get in the ideal soccer shape and increment your continuance too. The capacity to go for vast periods is continuance, and this is fundamental for being effective at soccer.

In this way, feel free to agree to accept that soccer crew, after you've attempted the above strength training exercises to make you a great player. By structure, your strength and your stamina you can build your

Rules for Parents

INTRODUCTION

If you want your child to come out of his youth sports experience a winner (feeling good about himself and having a healthy attitude towards sports), then he needs your help! You are a vital and important part of the coach-athlete-parent team. If you do your job correctly and play your position well, then your child will learn the sport faster, perform better, really have fun and have his self-esteem enhanced as a result. His sport experience will serve as a positive model for him to follow as he approaches other challenges and obstacles throughout life.

If you "drop the ball" or run the wrong way with it, your child will stop learning, experience performance difficulties and blocks, and begin to really hate the sport. And that's the good news! Further, your relationship with him will probably suffer significantly. As a result, he will come out of this experience burdened with feelings of failure, inadequacy and low self-esteem, feelings that will generalize to other areas in his life. Your child and his coach need you on the team. They can't win without you! The following are a list of useful facts, guidelines and strategies for you to use to make you more skilled in the youth sport game. Remember, no wins unless everyone wins. We need you on the team

STEP ONE

When defined the right way, competition in youth sports is both good and healthy and teaches children a variety of important life skills. The word "compete" comes from the Latin words "com" and "petere" which mean together and seeking respectively. The true definition of competition is a seeking together where your opponent is your partner, not the enemy! The better he performs, the more chance you have of having a peak performance. Sports is about learning to deal with challenges and obstacles. Without a worthy opponent, without any challenges sports is not so much fun. The more the challenge the better the opportunity you have to go beyond your limits. World records are consistently broken and set at the Olympics because the best athletes in the world are "seeking together", challenging each other to enhanced performance.

STEP TWO

ENCOURAGE YOUR CHILD TO COMPETE AGAINST HIMSELF
The ultimate goal of the sport experience is to challenge oneself and continually improve. Unfortunately, judging improvement by winning and losing is both an unfair and inaccurate measure.

Winning in sports is about doing the best you can do, separate from the outcome or the play of your opponent. Children should be encouraged to compete against their own potential (i.e., Peter and Patty Potential). That is, the boys should focus on beating "Peter", competing against themselves, while the girls challenge "Patty". When your child has this focus and plays to better himself instead of beating someone else, he will be more relaxed, have more fun and therefore perform better

STEP THREE

DO NOT DEFINE SUCCESS AND FAILURE IN TERMS OF WINNING AND LOSING A corollary to TWO, one of the main purposes of the youth sports experience is skill acquisition and mastery. When a child performs to his potential and loses it is criminal to focus on the outcome and become critical. If a child plays his very best and loses, you need to help him feel like a winner! Similarly, when a child or team performs far below their potential but wins, this is not cause to feel like a winner. Help your child make this important separation between success and failure and winning and losing. Remember, if you define success and failure in terms of winning and losing, you're playing a losing game with your child!

STEP FOUR

BE SUPPORTIVE, DO NOT COACH! Your role on the parent-coach-athlete team is as a Support player with a capital S! You need to be your child's best fan. unconditionally! Leave the coaching and instruction to the coach. Provide encouragement, support, empathy, transportation, money, help with fund-raisers, etc., but... do not coach! Most parents that get into trouble with their children do so because they forget to remember the important position that they play.

Coaching interferes with your role as supporter and fan. The last thing your child needs and wants to hear from you after a disappointing performance or loss is what they did technically or strategically wrong. Keep your role as a parent on the team separate from that as coach, and, if by necessity you actually get stuck in the almost no-win position of having to coach your child, try to maintain this separation of roles (i.e. on the deck, field or court say, "Now I'm talking to you as a coach", at home say, "Now I'm talking to you as a parent"). Don't parent when you coach and don't coach at home when you're supposed to be parenting.

STEP FIVE

HELP MAKE THE SPORT FUN FOR YOUR CHILD It's a time proven principle of peak performance that the more fun an athlete is having, the more they will learn and the better they will perform. Fun must be present for peak performance to happen at every level of sports from youth to world class competitor! When a child stops having fun and begins to dread practice or competition, it's time for you as a parent to become concerned! When the sport or game becomes too serious, athletes have a tendency to burn out and become susceptible to repetitive performance problems.

An easy rule of thumb: If your child is not enjoying what they are doing, nor loving the heck out of it, investigate! What is going on that's preventing them from having fun? Is it the coaching? The pressure? Is it you?! Keep in mind that being in a highly competitive program does not mean that there is no room for fun. The child that continues to play long after the fun is going will soon become a drop out statistic.

STEP SIX

WHOSE GOAL IS IT? FIVE leads us to a very important question! Why is your child participating in the sport? Are they doing it because they want to, for them, or because of you. When they have problems in their sport do you talk about them as "our" problems, "our jump isn't high enough", "we're having trouble with our flip turn" , etc. Are they playing because they don't want to disappoint you, because they know how important the sport is to you?

Are they playing for rewards and "bonuses" that you give out? Are their goals and aspirations yours or theirs? How invested are you in their success and failure? If they are competing to please you or for your vicarious glory they are in it for the wrong reasons! Further, if they stay involved for you, ultimately everyone will lose. It is quite normal and healthy to want your child to excel and be as successful as possible. But, you cannot make this happen by pressuring them with your expectations or by using guilt or bribery to keep them involved. If they have their own reasons and own goals for participating, they will be far more motivated to excel and therefore far more successful.

STEP SEVEN

YOUR CHILD IS NOT HIS PERFORMANCE-LOVE HIM UNCONDITIONALLY Do not equate your child's self-worth and lovability with his performance. The most tragic and damaging mistake I see parents continually make is punishing a child for a bad performance by withdrawing emotionally from him. A child loses a race, strikes out or misses and easy shot on goal and the parent responds with disgust, anger and withdrawal of love and approval. CAUTION: Only use this strategy if you want to damage your child emotionally and ruin your relationship with him. In the 1988 Olympics, when Greg Louganis needed and got a perfect 10 on his last dive to overtake the Chinese diver for the gold medal, his last thought before he went was, "If I don't make it, my mother will still love me".

STEP EIGHT

REMEMBER THE IMPORTANCE OF SELF-ESTEEM IN ALL OF YOUR INTERACTIONS WITH YOUR CHILD-ATHLETE
Athletes of all ages and levels perform in direct relationship to how they feel about themselves. When your child is in an athletic environment that boosts his self-esteem, he will learn faster, enjoy himself more and perform better under competitive pressure. One thing we all want as children and never stop wanting is to be loved and accepted, and to have our parents feel good about what we do. This is how self-esteem gets established. When your interactions with your child make him feel good about himself, he will, in turn, learn to treat himself this very same way.

This does not mean that you have to incongruently compliment your child for a great effort after they have just performed miserably. In this situation being empathic and sensitive to his feelings is what's called for. Self esteem makes the world go round. Make your child feel good about himself and you've given him a gift that lasts a lifetime. Do not interact with your child in a way that assaults his self-esteem by degrading, embarrassing or humiliating him. If you continually put your child down or minimize his accomplishments not only will he learn to do this to himself throughout his life, but he will also repeat your mistake with his children!

STEP NINE

GIVE YOUR CHILD THE GIFT OF FAILURE If you really want your child to be as happy and as successful as possible in everything that he does, teach him how to fail! The most successful people in and out of sports do two things differently than everyone else. First,, they are more willing to take risks and therefore fail more frequently. Second, they use their failures in a positive way as a source of motivation and feedback to improve. Our society is generally negative and teaches us that failure is bad, a cause for humiliation and embarrassment, and something to be avoided at all costs.

Fear of failure or humiliation causes one to be tentative and non-active. In fact, most performance blocks and poor performances are a direct result of the athlete being preoccupied with failing or messing up. You can't learn to walk without falling enough times. Each time that you fall your body gets valuable information on how to do it better. You can't be successful or have peak performances if you are concerned with losing or failing. Teach your child how to view setbacks, mistakes and risk-taking positively and you'll have given him the key to a lifetime of success. Failure is the perfect stepping stone to success.

STEP TEN

CHALLENGE, DON'T THREATEN Many parents directly or indirectly use guilt and threats as a way to "motivate" their child to perform better. Performance studies clearly indicate that while threats may provide short term results, the long term costs in terms of psychological health and performance are devastating. Using fear as a motivator is probably one of the worst dynamics you could set up with your child.

Threats take the fun out of performance and directly lead to your child performing terribly. implicit in a threat, (do this or else!) is your own anxiety that you do not believe the child is capable. Communicating this lack of belief, even indirectly is further devastating to the child's performance. A challenge does not entail loss or negative consequences should the athlete fail. Further, implicit in a challenge is the empowering belief, "I think that you can do it".

STEP ELEVEN

STRESS PROCESS, NOT OUTCOME When athletes choke under pressure and perform far below their potential, a very common cause of this is a focus on the outcome of the performance (i.e., win/lose, instead of the process). In any peak performance, the athlete is totally oblivious to the outcome and instead is completely absorbed in the here and now of the actual performance.

An outcome focus will almost always distract and tighten up the athlete insuring a bad performance. Furthermore focusing on the outcome, which is completely out of the athlete's control will raise his anxiety to a performance inhibiting level. So if you truly want your child to win, help get his focus away from how important the contest is and have them focus on the task at hand. Supportive parents de-emphasize winning and instead stress learning the skills and playing the game.

STEP TWELVE

AVOID COMPARISONS AND RESPECT DEVELOPMENTAL DIFFERENCES Supportive parents do not use other athletes that their child competes against to compare and thus evaluate their child's progress. Comparisons are useless, inaccurate and destructive. Each child matures differently and the process of comparison ignores significant distorting effects of developmental differences.

For example, two 12 year old boys may only have their age in common! One may physically have the build and perform like a 16 year old while the other, a late developer, may have the physical size and attribute of a 9 year old. Performance comparisons can prematurely turn off otherwise talented athletes on their sport. The only value of comparisons is in teaching. If one child demonstrates proper technique, that child can be used comparatively as a model only! For your child to do his very best he needs to learn to stay within himself. Worrying about how another athlete is doing interferes with him doing this.

Activity for Children and Adolescents

Identify the benefits of regular physical activity among youth

•Describe the key physical activity guidelines for children and adolescents

• Describe the role of communities in promoting physical activity among children and adolescents

A Day in the Life for kids

Walks to and from school

- Jumps rope and does gymnastics in physical education class

- Plays on the playground during recess

- Does homework

- Watches television

- Plays soccer with family

- Plays video games

How Does Physical Activity Help?

Promotes health and fitness
- Builds healthy bones and muscles[1]

- Reduces the risk of developing obesity and risk factors for diseases such as type 2 diabetes and heart disease[1]

- Reduces the symptoms of anxiety and depression[1]

- Can positively affect concentration, memory, and classroom behavior[2]

How Much Physical Activity should our Youth do?

Children and adolescents should do 60 minutes (1 hour) or more of physical activity daily. ⬚ Aerobic Activities: Most of the 60 or more minutes per day should be either moderate- or vigorous-intensity aerobic physical activity. Include vigorous-intensity physical activity at least 3 days per week.

Muscle-strengthening Activities: Include muscle-strengthening physical activity on at least 3 days of the week, as part of the 60 or more minutes. ⬚ Bone-strengthening Activities: Include bone-strengthening physical activity on at least 3 days of the week, as part of the 60 or more minutes. • Activities should be age-appropriate, enjoyable, and offer variety.

Sports Injuries and your Child

Ankle sprain: aftercare

There are 3 grades of ankle sprains:

Grade I sprains: Your ligaments are stretched. It is a mild injury that can improve with some light stretching.
Grade II sprains: Your ligaments are partially torn. You may need to wear a splint or a cast.

Grade III sprains: Your ligaments are fully torn. You may need surgery for this severe injury.

The last 2 kinds of sprains are often associated with tearing of small blood vessels. This allows blood to leak into tissues and cause black and blue color in the area. The blood may not appear for several days. Most of the time, it is absorbed from the tissues within 2 weeks.

If your sprain is more severe:
You may feel strong pain and have a lot of swelling.
You may not be able to walk, or walking may be painful.
Some ankle sprains may become chronic (long-lasting). If this happens to you, your ankle may continue to be:
Painful and swollen, Weak or giving way easily

What to Expect

Your health care provider may order an x-ray to look for a bone fracture, or an MRI scan to look for an injury to the ligament.

To help your ankle heal, your provider may treat you with a brace, a cast, or a splint, and may give you crutches to walk on. You may be asked to place only part or none of your weight on the bad ankle. You will also need to do physical therapy or exercises to help you recover from the injury.

Getting Active

The pain and swelling of an ankle sprain most often gets better within 48 hours. After that, you can begin to put weight back on your injured foot. Put only as much weight on your foot as is comfortable at first. Slowly work your way up to your full weight. If your ankle begins to hurt, stop and rest. Your provider will give you exercises to strengthen your foot and ankle. Doing these exercises can help prevent future sprains and chronic ankle pain. For less severe sprains, you may be able to go back to your normal activities after a few days. For more severe sprains, it may take several weeks.

Elbow sprain - aftercare

A sprain is an injury to the ligaments around a joint. A ligament is a band of tissue that connects bone to bone. The ligaments in your elbow help connect the bones of your upper and lower arm around your elbow joint. When you sprain your elbow, you have pulled or torn one or more of the ligaments in your elbow joint.

More About The Injury

An elbow sprain can occur when your arm is quickly bent or twisted in an unnatural position. It can also happen when the ligaments are overloaded during regular movement. Elbow sprains can happen when:

You fall with your arm stretched out, such as when playing sports, or your elbow is hit very hard, such as during a car accident

What to Expect

You may notice:

Elbow pain and swelling bruising, redness, or warmth around your elbow. Pain when you move your elbow. Tell your doctor if you heard a "pop" when you injured your elbow. This could be a sign that the ligament was torn. After examining your elbow, your doctor may order an x-ray to see if there are any breaks (fractures) to the bones in your elbow. You may also have an MRI of the elbow. The MRI pictures will show whether tissues around your elbow have been stretched or torn. If you have an elbow sprain, you may need, a sling to keep your arm and elbow from moving. A cast or splint if you have severe sprain

Activity

You may need to wear a sling, splint, or cast for about 2 to 3 weeks while your elbow heals. Depending on how badly it is sprained, you may need to work with a physical therapist who will show you stretching and strengthening exercises. Most people recover completely from a simple elbow sprain in about 4 weeks.

Foot sprain - aftercare

There are many bones and ligaments in your foot. A ligament is a strong flexible tissue that holds bones together. When the foot lands awkwardly, some ligaments can stretch and tear. This is called a sprain. When the injury occurs to the middle part of the foot, this is called a mid-foot sprain.

More about the Injury

Most foot sprains happen due to sports or activities in which your body twists and pivots but your feet stay in place. Some of these sports include football, snowboarding, and dance. There are three levels of foot sprains. Grade I, minor. You have small tears in the ligaments. Grade II, moderate. You have large tears in the ligaments. Grade III, severe. The ligaments are completely disrupted or detached from the bone.

CONCLUSION

If you are a youth soccer player, at that point, you might search for an approach to improve your soccer shot. In all honesty, there are a few diverse ways that you can improve your soccer shot if you are a youth soccer player. Most players don't understand this; however, if you need to show signs of improvement at shoot the ball, you are merely going to need to rehearse. Appropriate discipline brings about promising results particularly with regards to shooting the ball. A champion among the most critical things that you have to do when firing a shot is to utilize the proper technique. If you don't use appropriate technology when shooting the ball, at that point, you will never have the capacity to score an objective with regards to a first soccer match-up.

never have the capacity to score an objective with regards to a first soccer match-up.

When attempting to improve your shot, it is additionally critical for you to have the capacity to take a volley shot. A volleyed chance is a shot that is made in mid-air. There are a few distinctive ways that you can rehearse your volley shot for soccer. A standout amongst the ideal approaches to rehearse your volley shot is to juggle the ball three to multiple times and after that to make a go after your last juggle. This will enable you to effectively rehearse your volley shot and get ready to make a go in a genuine diversion. In any case, if you need to show signs of improvement at shooting the ball, at that point, you are going to need to work on shooting on an open net once a day. If you can work on shooting on a goalkeeper, at that point, you ought to do that as opposed to shooting on an open net! Just recall, continue rehearsing!

Medical References

Molloy A, Selvan D. Ligamentous injuries of the foot and ankle. In: Miller MD, Thompson SR, eds. *DeLee and Drez's Orthopaedic Sports Medicine*. 4th ed. Philadelphia, PA: Elsevier Saunders; 2015:chap 116. Rose NGW, Green TJ. Ankle and foot. In: Walls RM, Hockberger RS, Gausche-Hill M, eds. *Rosen's Emergency Medicine: Concepts and Clinical Practice*. 9th ed. Philadelphia, PA: Elsevier; 2018:chap 51

Disclosure Statement

Disclosure Statement
All information and content contained in this book are provided solely for general information and reference purposes. SSP LLC Limited makes no statement, representation, warranty or guarantee as to the accuracy, reliability or timeliness of the information and content contained in this Book.

Neither SSP Limited or the author of this book nor any of its related company accepts any responsibility or liability for any direct or indirect loss or damage, injury prevention (whether in tort, contract or otherwise) which may be suffered or occasioned by any person howsoever arising due to any inaccuracy, omission, misrepresentation or error in respect of any information and content provided by this book (including any third-party books.

Workout Notes

Workout Notes

Workout Notes

Workout Notes

Workout Notes

Workout Notes

Workout Notes

Workout Notes

S.S. Publishing

Printed in Great Britain
by Amazon